/ 12/17 (0)

WEIGH It!

RACHEL FIRST

Consulting Editor, Diane Craig, M.A./Reading Specialist

Sandcastle

An Imprint of Abdo Publishing
abdopublishing.com

abdopublishing.com

Published by Abdo Publishing, a division of ABDO, PO Box 398166, Minneapolis, Minnesota 55439. Copyright © 2016 by Abdo Consulting Group, Inc. International copyrights reserved in all countries. No part of this book may be reproduced in any form without written permission from the publisher. SandCastle™ is a trademark and logo of Abdo Publishing.

Printed in the United States of America, North Mankato, Minnesota
102015
012016

Editor: Liz Salzmann
Content Developer: Nancy Tuminelly
Cover and Interior Design and Production: Mighty Media, Inc.
Photo Credits: Shutterstock

Library of Congress Cataloging-in-Publication Data

First, Rachel, author.
 Weigh it! : fun with weight / Rachel First ; consulting editor, Diane Craig, M.A./reading specialist.
    pages cm. -- (Math beginnings)
 ISBN 978-1-62403-936-2
1. Weights and measures--Juvenile literature. 2. Weight (Physics)--Measurement--Juvenile literature. 3. Mathematics--Juvenile literature. I. Title.
 QC90.6.F57 2016
 530.8'1--dc23
                    2015020861

SandCastle™ Level: Transitional

SandCastle™ books are created by a team of professional educators, reading specialists, and content developers around five essential components—phonemic awareness, phonics, vocabulary, text comprehension, and fluency—to assist young readers as they develop reading skills and strategies and increase their general knowledge. All books are written, reviewed, and leveled for guided reading, early reading intervention, and Accelerated Reader™ programs for use in shared, guided, and independent reading and writing activities to support a balanced approach to literacy instruction. The SandCastle™ series has four levels that correspond to early literacy development. The levels are provided to help teachers and parents select appropriate books for young readers.

EMERGING · BEGINNING · **TRANSITIONAL** · FLUENT

Contents

WEIGHT
All Around

Look around you!

All things have weight. Weight is how heavy something is.

Weighing
things
is fun!

Alex is at
the store.
She gets
apples.
She weighs
them.

SCALES

We weigh
things on
scales.

The scale shows a number. That is the weight.

There are different scales. Kitchen scales weigh food. Bathroom scales weigh people.

Which SYSTEM?

Two systems measure weight.

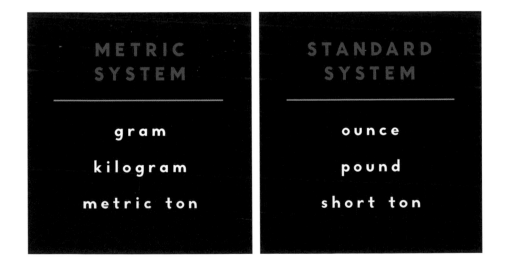

METRIC SYSTEM	STANDARD SYSTEM
gram	ounce
kilogram	pound
metric ton	short ton

Most countries use the metric system. The United States uses the standard system.

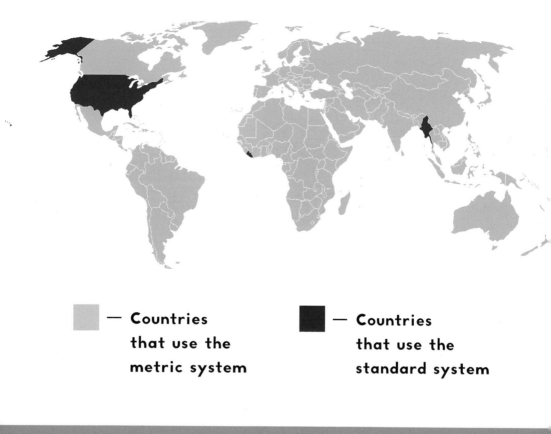

Countries that use the metric system

Countries that use the standard system

Can You CARRY IT?

Many things are light. They are easy to carry. We weigh them in grams and ounces.

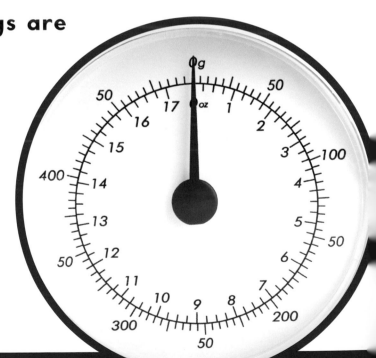

Dan has
a dollar
bill. It
weighs
1 gram.

Ellie has
a pencil.
It is red.
It weighs
1 ounce.

We weigh heavier things in pounds and kilograms.

Brian loves bananas! He eats one every day.

Three bananas weigh about one pound.

Six bananas weigh about one kilogram.

You can carry these. Just make sure there aren't too many!

Short tons and metric tons are large weights. They are about **equal** to each other.

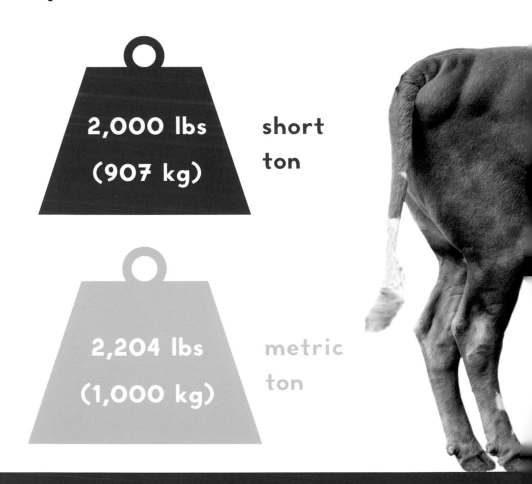

2,000 lbs
(907 kg)

short ton

2,204 lbs
(1,000 kg)

metric ton

A large
bull weighs
about
one ton.

You
can't
carry a
bull!

LIGHT or HEAVY?

Are big things heavy? Are small things light? Not always!

Mara has a big beach ball. It is light.

Ivan has
a bowling
ball. It is
smaller. But
it is heavy.

Try It!

Find two
things about
the same
size. Lift
both. Is one
heavier?

What other things are big but light?

What things are small but heavy?

PRACTICE

Look at the pictures on the right.

Try to name them in order from lightest to heaviest.

What would be the best way to weigh each one? Think about it. Then follow the lines with your finger. Were you right?

short
tons or
metric
tons

ounces
or
grams

pounds
or
kilograms

Glossary

BILL — a piece of paper money, such as a one-dollar bill or a five-dollar bill.

BOWLING — a game in which you try to knock over pins by rolling a heavy ball down an alley.

DOLLAR — a unit of money. Prices are listed in dollar amounts.

EQUAL — having exactly the same size or amount.

SYSTEM — a way of doing something.